"The Exciting World of Fundo"
by Garry and Ayana Atkinson

© 2017, Fundo Press, LLC

Edited by Lakela Atkinson, www.ForTheLoveOfWordsOnline.com
ForTheLoveOfWords1@gmail.com

www.FundoPress.com

For my niece and goddaughter, Ayesha Quanette Sanders, Jr. May you be blessed with genius, strength, and a love for learning.

Love always,
Uncle Garry

For my parents who instilled a love of reading within me. For my future children, I hope I can give you the same gift.

Yannie

Welcome to my world!

Come with me on a journey.

I'll tell you about myself.

I live on the planet Saturn with my daddy and mommy.

We also live with our pet camel, Connie

like to play outside. My favorite sport

is tennis, which I play on a court.

like to read books and learn new things.

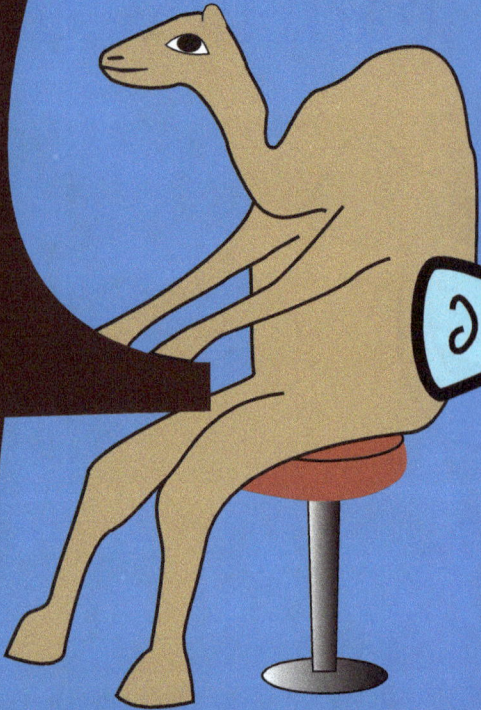

My shirt is red, and my skin is blue.

Now, it's your turn. Tell me about you.

My name is _____.

Write your name above.

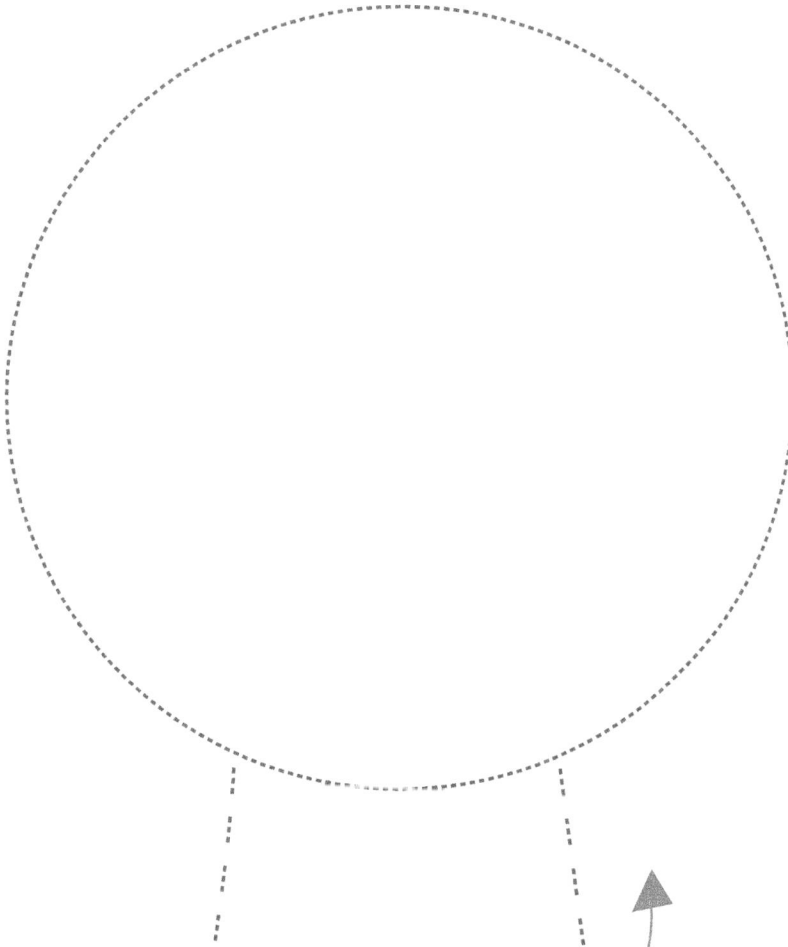

Draw your face here.

My _____ is _____.
My skin is _____.

Write about yourself and your outfit above

Draw your outfit here.

My father is a teacher of a class.

He teaches kids how to do math.

1
+2

My mother is a space cadet.

She explores space and other planets.

Every summer my parents travel to Earth.

I'm so excited, this trip is my first.

Since Earth is a different planet,

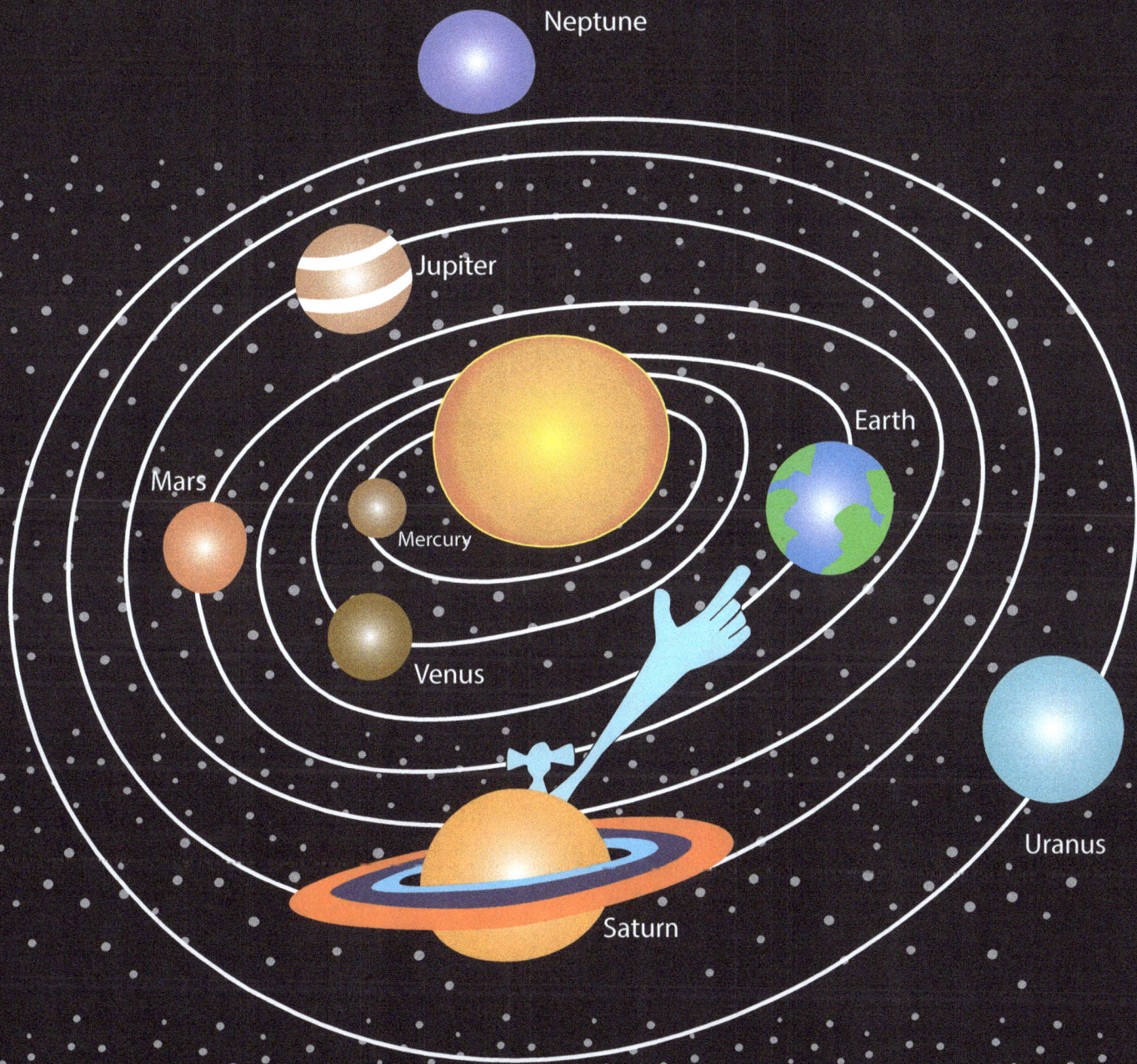

we will travel there in a spaceship.

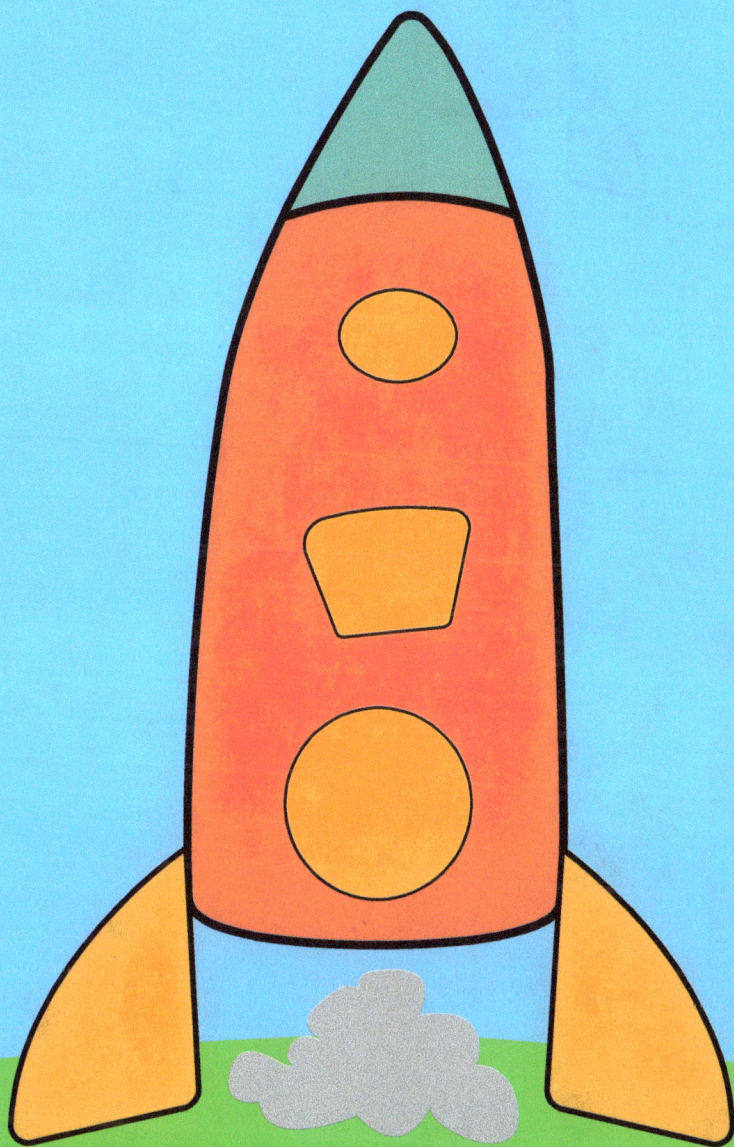

The spaceship is built to fly

way up high and past the sky.

t travels through space like planes and cars.

The spaceship takes us to the stars.

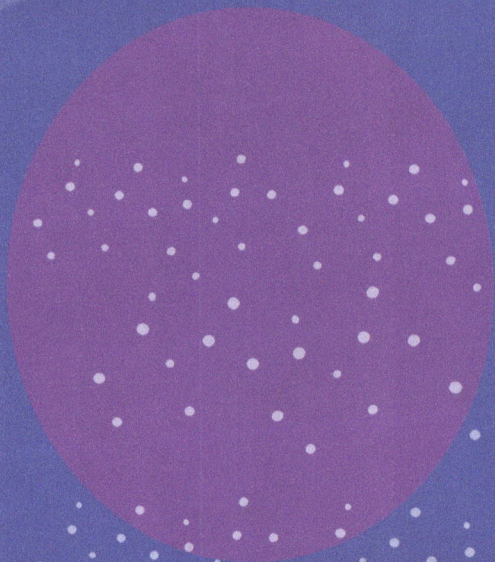

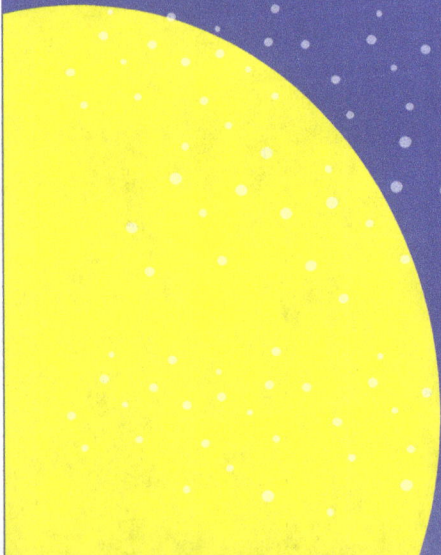

When we reach the Earth's landing strip,

we will begin our family trip.

There is so much to do at every turn.

Read more of my books if you want to learn

Thanks for joining Fundo on his journey to Earth!

See you next time.

Have fun learning!

We would like to sincerely thank you for your reading with Fundo!

Sincerely,
Garry & Ayana Atkinson
Co-Authors

For more books and products, please visit www.FundoPress.com

Please look for the following books in the Fundo Press family:

Available now:
        "Fundo's Animal Alphabet"

Coming Soon:

        "Fundo's Telling Time"
        "Fundo's 123 Counting"
        "Fundo's Shape Story"
        "Fundo's Vegetable Voyage"

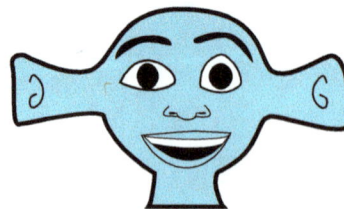

FUNDO
PRESS

www.ingramcontent.com/pod-product-compliance
Lightning Source LLC
Chambersburg PA
CBHW081539040426
42447CB00014B/3440